THE

IMMATURE
BOOK CLUB

Self published, London, England
First printed February 2015
Copyright ©2016 The Immature Book Club
All rights reserved

"The Book of Foreign Swear Words" by **The Immature Book Club**
ISBN-13: 978-1541077300 • ISBN-10: 154107730X

Author's Note
This book is not to be taken seriously. However the characters, places and incidents either are the products of our imagination or are used fictitiously, and any resemblance to actual persons, living or dead, events, or locales is entirely coincidental.

CONTENTS

DEAR READER,

WE HOPE YOU ENJOY THIS WASTE OF SPACE BOOK.

THIS HAS PROBABLY BEEN GIVEN TO YOU AS A PRANK OR YOU MAY

HAVE PURCHASED THIS TO IMPROVE YOUR MULTILINGUAL SKILLS!

EITHER WAY, THIS BOOK IS EITHER GOING TO BRING YOU JOY OR A

BLACK-EYE.

OH AND FOR THOSE OF YOU 'SERIOUS' FOLKS WITH NO

SENSE OF HUMOUR - CHILL THE **FUCK** OUT!

_____

THE IMMATURE BOOK CLUB.

@IMMATUREBC

#FOREIGNSWEARWORDS

HOW TO SWEAR IN
ENGLISH

"FUCK"

[VARIATIONS INCLUDE:
"FUCKING" AND "FUCKER"]

IT'S A VERY DIVERSE WORD. IT CAN BE USED A SWEAR WORD BY ITSELF OR AS AN EXPRESSION OF EXCITEMENT.

EXAMPLES :

"FUCK OFF!" = GO AWAY!

"OH FUCK!" = EXCITEMENT OR SHOCK WORD

"CUNT"

[DEFINITION:

"VAGINA/PUSSY"]

THIS IS SOMETHING YOU SAY IF YOU WANT TO GET SERIOUSLY BEATEN UP OR LOSE SOME FRIENDS. FOR SOME STRANGE REASON IT HOLDS SO MUCH WEIGHT COMPARED TO ANY OTHER SWEAR WORD.

EXAMPLE:

"YOU'RE A CUNT" = SELF-EXPLANATORY

"TWAT"

[DEFINITION:

"A PRETTY STUPID INDIVIDUAL"]

EXAMPLE:

"HE'S A PROPER TWAT!" = HE'S REALLY STUPID!

"PISS OFF!"

[
DEFINITION:
"QUITE SIMILAR TO THE TERM 'FUCK'"
]

SOME PEOPLE USE IT AS A "GO AWAY!" TERM BUT IT
COULD ALSO BE USED TO EXPRESS SHOCK.

EXAMPLE:

"PISS OFF!" = GO AWAY!

"BITCH / BASTARD"

[
DEFINITION:
"A DESPICABLE PERSON"
]

EXAMPLE:

SIMPLY PLUG WHERE APPROPRIATE, BITCH!

"SLUT / HOE / WHORE / SKANK"

[VARIATIONS INCLUDE:

"A PROMISCUOUS INDIVIDUAL"]

YOU CAN CALL A WOMAN EITHER OF THESE NAMES IF YOU WANT TO MAKE THEM FEEL CHEAP, WORTHLESS OR IF YOU'RE JUST TRYING TO EXPRESS HOW PROMISCUOUS YOU THINK THEY ARE.

EXAMPLE:

"YOU SLUT!" = SELF-EXPLANATORY

HOW TO SWEAR IN
FRENCH

"MERDE!"

[
DEFINITION: "SHIT!"

PRONOUNCED: "MAIRD"
]

USED FOR EXTRA EMPHASIS. YOU'LL HEAR PEOPLE SAY "MAIR-DUUHHH" INSTEAD OF THE MORE ACCURATE "MAIRD".

"PUTAIN / PUTE"

[
DEFINITION: "WHORE!"

PRONOUNCED: "POO-TAHN" / "POOTE"
]

USE WITH CAUTION! THIS TENDS TO BE USED AS AN EMOTIONAL REACTION TO SOMETHING, LIKE "FUCK!" YOU CAN ALSO DIRECT IT AT SOMEONE IN PARTICULAR - "A PUTE" (THAT WHORE). PEOPLE JOKE THAT THE WORD "FUCK" CAN BE USED IN EVERY PART OF SPEECH IN ENGLISH. IN FRENCH, "PUTAIN" FUNCTIONS PRETTY MUCH THE SAME WAY.

"SALOPE / SALOP"

[
DEFINITION: "BITCH!"

PRONOUNCED: "SAL-<u>OPE</u>" OR "SAL-<u>OH</u>" (MASCULINE)
]

YOU'LL MOST LIKELY BE DIRECTING THIS ONE AT SOMEONE IN PARTICULAR, RATHER THAN AS AN ANGRY SWEAR WORD SHOUTED IN RESPONSE TO SOMETHING. IT IS USED PRETTY MUCH EXACTLY THE SAME WAY THE WORD IS USED IN ENGLISH. ALSO, LIKE IN ENGLISH, YOU CAN INCORPORATE THIS WORD INTO A PHRASE LIKE – "FILS DE SALOPE" (SON OF A BITCH).

"CHIANT / ÇA ME FAIT CHIER"

[
DEFINITION: "THAT PISSES ME OFF!"

PRONOUNCED: "<u>CHI</u>-ANT" / "SA MEH FEY <u>CHIAY</u>"
]

USED IN THE CONTEXT OF "ÇA ME FAIT CHIER" MEANS A BAD VERSION OF "THAT PISSES ME OFF!"

"FOUTRE / JE M'EN FOU"

[
DEFINITION: FOUTRE -"FUCK"

PRONOUNCED: "FOO-TRUH / JUH MEN FOO"
]

USE WITH CAUTION AS "FOUTRE" IS THE VERB FOR "TO FUCK." YOU'LL HEAR THIS IN THE PHRASE "JE M'EN FOU" WHICH MEANS "I DON'T GIVE A FUCK.

"CHIANT / ÇA ME FAIT CHIER"

[
DEFINITION: "THAT PISSES ME OFF!"

PRONOUNCED: "CHI-ANT" / "SA MEH FEY CHIAY"
]

USED IN THE CONTEXT OF "ÇA ME FAIT CHIER" MEANS A BAD VERSION OF "THAT PISSES ME OFF!"

"CON / CONASSE / CONNARD"

[
DEFINITION: "ASS / IDIOT"
PRONOUNCED: "COHN / CON-<u>ASS</u> / CON-<u>ARD</u>"
]

USED AS "ASS" IN FRENCH BUT SOMETIMES TRANSLATED AS A MILDER "IDIOT."

"NIQUE TA MERE!"

[
DEFINITION: "FUCK YOUR MOTHER!"
PRONOUNCED: "NEEK TAH MARE"
]

THIS PHRASE SHOULD BE RESERVED FOR SITUATIONS WHEN ONLY THE MOST EXTREME SWEAR IS NEEDED.

"TA GUEULE!"

[DEFINITION: "SHUT UP!"
PRONOUNCED: "TA-GOOL"]

A RUDE WAY TO SAY SHUT UP. BUT USED AMONGST
FRIENDS WHEN MESSING AROUND.

"CASSE-TOI!"

[DEFINITION: "PISS OR FUCK OFF!"
PRONOUNCED: "KASS-TWAH!"]

COMBINED WITH ANOTHER SWEAR WORD LIKE "CON", IT
CAN ACTUALLY PACK QUITE A POWERFUL PUNCH!

"TA GUEULE!"

[DEFINITION: "SHUT UP!"

PRONOUNCED: "TA-GOOL"]

A RUDE WAY TO SAY SHUT UP. BUT USED AMONGST
FRIENDS WHEN MESSING AROUND.

"CASSE-TOI!"

[DEFINITION: "PISS OR FUCK OFF!"

PRONOUNCED: "KASS-TWAH!"]

COMBINED WITH ANOTHER SWEAR WORD LIKE "CON", IT
CAN ACTUALLY PACK QUITE A POWERFUL PUNCH!

"C'EST DES CONNERIES!"

[DEFINITION: "THIS IS BULLSHIT!"]
[PRONOUNCED: "SAY-DAY-KOHN-REE!"]

THROW IN EXTRA WORDS FOR EMPHASIS LIKE "C'EST VRAIMENT DES CONNERIES!" (THAT IS REALLY BULLSHIT).

HOW TO SWEAR IN
SPANISH

INCLUDING: SOUTH AMERICAN AND ARGENTINIAN SPANISH

"CABRON!"

[DEFINITION: "FUCKING BASTARD!"]

"GILIPOLLAS / TONTOPOLLAS"

[DEFINITION: "DICKHEAD / ASSHOLE"]

"PICHACORTA"

[DEFINITION: "LITTLE DICK"]

"COÑO / CHOCHO / RAJA"

[DEFINITION: "CUNT / PUSSY"]

"CHICHI"

[DEFINITION: "PUSSY"]

"PELOS DE LOS HUEVOS"

[DEFINITION: "PUBIC HAIR"]

"MIERDA!"

[DEFINITION: "SHIT!"]

"CHUPAME LA POLLA!"

[DEFINITION: "SUCK MY DICK!"]

"CHUPAMELA!"

[DEFINITION: "SUCK IT"]

"PUTA"

[DEFINITION: "BITCH/WHORE"]

"ZORRA / GUARRA"

[DEFINITION: "FOX / DIRTY GIRL"]

"ME CAGO EN TI!"

[DEFINITION: "I SHIT ON YOU!"]

"CHORRA / PINNUS"

[DEFINITION: "STUPID"]

"QUE TE JODAN!"

[DEFINITION: "FUCK YOU!"]

"PAYASO"

[DEFINITION: "CLOWN"]

"DESGRACIADO"

[DEFINITION: "UNLUCKY / SON OF A BITCH"]

"ME CAGO EN LA HOSTIA!"

[DEFINITION: "FUCKING DAMN IT!"]

"ME CAGO EN LA LECHE!"

[DEFINITION: "I SHIT IN THE MILK!" / "SHIT, I'VE HAVE BAD LUCK"]

"HIJO DE MIL PUTAS!"

[DEFINITION: "SON OF THOUSAND BITCHES!"]

"METETE UN PALO POR EL CULO!"

[DEFINITION: "SHOVE A STICK UP YOUR ASS!"]

"HUELES A MIERDA!"

[DEFINITION: "YOU SMELL LIKE SHIT"]

"JODE A TU MADRE!"

[DEFINITION: "FUCK YOUR MOTHER!"]

SOUTH AMERICAN SPANISH

"PINGA"

[DEFINITION: "DICK"]

"CHILITO"

[DEFINITION: "LITTLE DICK"]

"PANOCHA / CHIMBA"

[DEFINITION: "PUSSY / PUSSY (COLOMBIAN)"]

"CHINGA TU MADRE!"

[DEFINITION: "FUCK YOUR MOTHER!"]

"CAGO EN TU LECHE!"

[DEFINITION: "I SHIT IN YOUR MILK!"]

"PINCHE CABRON!"

[DEFINITION: "FUCKING SON OF A BITCH! (NOT LITERAL)"]

ARGENTINIAN SPANISH

"CONCHA"
[DEFINITION: "BITCH"]

"LA PIJA / VERGA"
[DEFINITION: "DICK"]

"EL ORTO / OJETE"
[DEFINITION: "ASS"]

"CHUPAME LA PIJA!"
[DEFINITION: "SUCK MY DICK!"]

"LAS TETAS"
[DEFINITION: "BOOBS"]

HOW TO SWEAR IN
FINNISH

"VITTU"

[DEFINITION: "FUCK / CUNT"]

"VITTUUN"

[DEFINITION: "FUCK OFF"]

"VITTUMAINEN"

[DEFINITION: "FUCKING CUNT"]

"VITTUPÄÄ"

[DEFINITION: "CUNTHEAD"]

"KUSIPÄÄ"

[DEFINITION: "PISSHEAD"]

"PASKIAINEN"

[DEFINITION: "BASTARD"]

"PASKA"

[DEFINITION: "SHIT"]

"SUKSI VITTUUN"

[DEFINITION: "SKI INTO A CUNT"]

"VEDÄ VITTU PÄÄHÄS!"

[DEFINITION: "DRAW A CUNT OVER YOUR HEAD!"]

"IME MUNAA, RUNKKARI"

[DEFINITION: "SUCK COCK, WANKER!"]

"ÄITISI NAI POROJA!"

[DEFINITION: "YOUR MOTHER COPULATES WITH REINDEER!"]

"PIMPPI"

[DEFINITION: "PUSSY"]

"MOLOPÄÄ!"

[DEFINITION: "DICKHEAD!"]

"HAISTA VITTU"

[DEFINITION: "SMELLY CUNT"]

"VEDÄ KÄTEEN"

[DEFINITION: "JERK OFF"]

"ISÄS OLI PUKKI / RUNKKU / KYVYTÖN, KUN SUA TEKI"

[DEFINITION: "YOUR DAD WAS A BUCK / WANKER / UNABLE WHEN HE MADE YOU"]

"PUKKI"

[DEFINITION: "A VERY VIRILE PERSON"]

"PASKAPÄÄ"

[DEFINITION: "SHITHEAD"]

"LUUSERI"

[DEFINITION: "LOSER / SUCKER"]

HOW TO SWEAR IN
DUTCH

"LUL"

[DEFINITION: "DICK"]

"KUT"

[DEFINITION: "CUNT"]

"KAK / STRONT / SCHIJT"

[DEFINITION: "SHIT"]

"REETNEUKER"

[DEFINITION: "ASS-FUCKER"]

"EIKEL"

[DEFINITION: "DICKHEAD"]

"HOER"

[DEFINITION: "HOOKER"]

"MOEDERNEUKER"

[DEFINITION: "MOTHERFUCKER"]

"RUKKER"

[DEFINITION: "WANKER"]

"SUKKEL"

[DEFINITION: "DUMB FUCK"]

"PIK OMHOOG"

[DEFINITION: "STIFF PRICK"]

"HOUD JE ROTSMOEL!"

[DEFINITION: "SHUT THE HELL UP!"]

"APENAAIER"

[DEFINITION: "MONKEY FUCKER"]

"DROOGKLOOT"

[DEFINITION: "BORING FUCK"]

"SUFKUT"

[DEFINITION: "BORING BITCH"]

"HOERENJONG"

[DEFINITION: "SON OF A BITCH / HOOKER"]

"JE MOEDER!"

[DEFINITION: "YOUR MOTHER! (USED AS A RESPONSE)"]

"KUTWIJF"

[DEFINITION: "CUNT / BITCH"]

"ZAKKEWASSER"

[DEFINITION: "TESTICLE WASHER"]

"PAARDENLUL"

[DEFINITION: "HORSEDICK"]

"SCHIJTLUL"

[DEFINITION: "SHITDICK"]

"ENGERD"

[DEFINITION: "CREEP"]

"SLET"

[DEFINITION: "SLUT"]

"HOEREJONG"

[DEFINITION: "SON OF A WHORE"]

"HONDELUL"

[DEFINITION: "DOG DICK"]

"LEEGHOOFD"

[DEFINITION: "AIRHEAD"]

"PIKHOOFD"

[DEFINITION: "COCKFACE"]

"TRUT"

[DEFINITION: "BITCH"]

"KUS MIJN KONT"

[DEFINITION: "KISS MY ASS"]

"STOMME LUL"

[DEFINITION: "STUPID DICK"]

"IK LAAT EEN SCHEET IN JOUW RICHTING!"

[DEFINITION: "I FART IN YOUR DIRECTION"]

"ENGERD"

[DEFINITION: "CREEP"]

"SLET"

[DEFINITION: "SLUT"]

"HOEREJONG"

[DEFINITION: "SON OF A WHORE"]

"HONDELUL"

[DEFINITION: "DOG DICK"]

"LEEGHOOFD"

[DEFINITION: "AIRHEAD"]

HOW TO SWEAR IN
ITALIAN

"PUTTANA"

[DEFINITION: "WHORE"]

"FUNGULA / SCOPA"

[DEFINITION: "FUCK"]

"MERDA!"

[DEFINITION: "SHIT!"]

"VAFFANCULO"

[DEFINITION: "GO FUCK YOURSELF"]

"NO SKUCHE ALA GATS!"

[DEFINITION: "WHAT THE FUCK DO YOU WANT FROM MY BALLS?"]

"PEZZO DI MERDA!"

[DEFINITION: "PIECE OF SHIT!"]

"FIGLIO DI PUTTANA"

[DEFINITION: "SON OF A WHORE"]

"CAZZO VAI VIA STRONZO!"

[DEFINITION: "SHIT, GET OUT OF HERE JERK!"]

"BOCCHINO"

[DEFINITION: "BLOW JOB"]

"CHE CAZZO!"

[DEFINITION: "YOU DICK!"]

"SCOPA TUA MAMMA!"

[DEFINITION: "FUCK YOUR MOTHER!"]

"FOTTI TUA MADRE!"

[DEFINITION: "FUCK YOUR MOTHER!"]

"MERDA!"

[DEFINITION: "SHIT!"]

"LI MORTACCI TUA!"

[DEFINITION: "TO YOUR DEAD RELATIVE!"]

"VAI A MORIRE AMMAZZATO!"

[DEFINITION: "GO AND DIE / GET MURDERED!"]

HOW TO SWEAR IN
RUSSIAN

"SOOKA!"

[DEFINITION: "BITCH / TRAITOR / WHORE!"]

"FUCK"

[DEFINITION: "YOB"]

"YOB TVOIU MAT'!"

[DEFINITION: "FUCK YOUR MOTHER!"]

"POSHOL NA KHUI!"

[DEFINITION: "FUCK OFF!"]

"POSHOL V ZHOPU!"

[DEFINITION: "FUCK OFF!"]

"K CHORTOO!"

[DEFINITION: "GO TO HELL!"]

"KOOSHITE GOVNO EE OOMEEITE!"

[DEFINITION: "EAT SHIT AND DIE!"]

"ZA-EBEES"

[DEFINITION: "STOP BITCHING"]

"GOVNO"

[DEFINITION: "SHIT"]

"BLIAD!"

[DEFINITION: "OH SHIT! / WHORE!"]

"KHUI"

[DEFINITION: "COCK"]

"PIZDA"

[DEFINITION: "CUNT"]

"SRAKA / MUDAK"

[DEFINITION: "AN ASS / ASSHOLE"]

"GOVNIUK"

[DEFINITION: "SHITHEAD"]

"KHUYESOS'"

[DEFINITION: "COCKSUCKER"]

HOW TO SWEAR IN
TURKISH

"SIKTIR LAN!"

[DEFINITION: "GET FUCKED!"]

"SIKTIR!"

[DEFINITION: "FUCK YOU!"]

"ANANI SIKERIM!"

[DEFINITION: "I'LL FUCK YOUR MOTHER!"]

"GOTVEREN"

[DEFINITION: "ASS-GIVER"]

"CHUKUMU YALA"

[DEFINITION: "SUCK MY DICK"]

"OROSS PUH"
[DEFINITION: "BITCH"]

"PUSHTT"
[DEFINITION: "PIMP"]

"GELLBOURRIA SALAK"
[DEFINITION: "COME OVER HERE WIMP"]

HOW TO SWEAR IN
NIGERIAN

"ASHEWO!"

[DEFINITION: "PROSTITUTE"]

"ASHEIRE"

[DEFINITION: "LOW-LIFE"]

"ODE OSHI!"

[DEFINITION: "STUPID FUCK!"]

"DOKO MI"

[DEFINITION: "SUCK MY DICK"]

"ARINDIN"

[DEFINITION: "IMBECILE"]

"ODE BURUKU"

[DEFINITION: "STUPID FOOL"]

"OMO ALE"

[DEFINITION: "BASTARD"]

"EWURE OSHI!"

[DEFINITION: "STUPID GOAT!"]

HOW TO SWEAR IN
SWAHILI

"BASHA"

[DEFINITION: "FUCKER"]

"FALA"

[DEFINITION: "STUPID"]

HOW TO SWEAR IN
AFRIKAANS

"EK WENS JOU VINGERS VERANDER IN VISHOEKE, EN JOU BALLE BEGIN TE JEUK!"

[DEFINITION: "I HOPE YOUR FINGERS CHANGE INTO FISHING HOOKS, AND YOU GET AN ITCH IN YOUR BALLS!"]

"FOK JOU, EET KAK EN VREK!"

[DEFINITION: "FUCK YOU, EAT SHIT AND DIE!"]

"BLIKSEM!"

[DEFINITION: "FUCK IT!"]

"DIE POES"

[DEFINITION: "THAT BASTARD"]

"DIEP IN DIE KAK"

[DEFINITION: "IN DEEP SHIT"]

"DOM DOOS!"

[DEFINITION: "DUMB PUSSY!"]

"DOMKOP"

[DEFINITION: "IDIOT"]

"GAAN FOK JOUSELF"

[DEFINITION: "GO FUCK YOURSELF"]

"GAAN KAK 'N AAP!"

[DEFINITION: "GO FUCK A MONKEY!"]

"GAAN KAK!"

[DEFINITION: "EAT SHIT!"]

"HOER"

[DEFINITION: "WHORE"]

"HOER NAAIER"

[DEFINITION: "SLUT FUCKER"]

"HOERKIND"

[DEFINITION: "SON OF A WHORE"]

"JOU DOOS!"

[DEFINITION: "YOU SHITHEAD!"]

HOW TO SWEAR IN JAPANESE

"SHINJIMAE!"

[DEFINITION: "GO TO HELL!"]

"SHINE!"

[DEFINITION: "DIE!"]

"SHINDE KUDASAI"

[DEFINITION: "PLEASE DIE"]

"SHINDE MO II YO!"

[DEFINITION: "IT WOULD BE JUST FINE IF YOU JUST DIED!"]

"KUSO KURAE!"

[DEFINITION: "EAT SHIT!"]

"YARIMAN"

[DEFINITION: "SLUT / WHORE"]

"SHINE!"

[DEFINITION: "DIE!"]

"DASAI"

[DEFINITION: "UNFASHIONABLE / LAME / NOT COOL"]

"BUSU"

[DEFINITION: "UGLY / YOU'RE UGLY / DOG" (REFERRING TO WOMEN)]

"GESU"

[DEFINITION: "UGLY" (REFERRING TO MEN)]

"DEBU"

[DEFINITION: "FATTY"]

"KUSO"

[DEFINITION: "SHIT"]

"KUSOTTARE"

[DEFINITION: "SHIT DRIP"]

"KISAMA"

[DEFINITION: "YOU BASTARD / MOTHERFUCKER"]

"SHINE MESUBUTA DOMO!"

[DEFINITION: "DIE YOU FEMALE PIG!"]

HOW TO SWEAR IN CHINESE

"TĀ MĀ DE"

[DEFINITION: "FUCK / SHIT / DAMN IT!"]

"CÀO NǏ MĀ!"

[DEFINITION: "FUCK YOUR MOTHER!"]

"WÁNG BĀ DÀN"

[DEFINITION: "SON OF A BITCH"]

"GŌNG GÒNG QÌ CHĒ"

[DEFINITION: "PUBLIC BUS" (REFERRING TO A WOMAN)]

"CHĪ SHǏ!"

[DEFINITION: "EAT SHIT!"]

HOW TO SWEAR IN ARABIC

"AL'AMA!"

[DEFINITION: "BLINDNESS!" (TYPICALLY USED LIKE "DAMN!")]

"SHARMOOTA"

[DEFINITION: "WHORE"]

"BIZ"

[DEFINITION: "TIT"]

"TEEZ"

[DEFINITION: "ASS"]

"KHARA!"

[DEFINITION: "SHIT!"]

"KIS IKHTAK!"

[DEFINITION: "YOUR SISTER'S VAGINA!" (TYPICALLY USED LIKE "FUCK!")]

"SHARMOOTA"

[DEFINITION: "WHORE"]

"YA IBN ASHARMOOTA!"

[DEFINITION: "YOU SON OF A WHORE!"]

"MUS ZIBBI"

[DEFINITION: "SUCK MY DICK"]

"ILHAS TEEZI"

[DEFINITION: "LICK MY ASS"]

"'AYRI FEEK"

[DEFINITION: "MY DICK IS IN YOU"]

"KUL KHARA"

[DEFINITION: "EAT SHIT"]

"TEEZAK HAMRA!"

[DEFINITION: "YOUR BUTT IS RED" (IN ENGLISH - "DUMBASS!")]

HOW TO SWEAR IN
THAI

"LOOG-GA-REE!"

[DEFINITION: "SON OF A BITCH!"]

"POR MUNG TAI / MAE-MUNG-TAI"

[DEFINITION: "WISH YOUR FATHER DEAD" / "WISH YOUR MOTHER DEAD"]

"YET POR!"

[DEFINITION: "FUCK YOUR FATHER!"]

"HEE MAE MANG!"

[DEFINITION: "FUCK YOUR MOTHER!"]

"MAE MUNG!"

[DEFINITION: "YO MOMMA!"]

"FARANG BA!"

[DEFINITION: "STUPID FOREIGNER!" (WE'VE ALL BEEN CALLED THIS)]

"YET"

[DEFINITION: "FUCK"]

"KUAY"

[DEFINITION: "COCK" (ALSO MEANS "BANANA")]

"KWAI!"

[DEFINITION: "BUFFALO" (ALSO MEANS "MOOOOO!" - DON'T ASK)]

"ORN KUAY"

[DEFINITION: "SUCK COCK"]

"I HAYER"

[DEFINITION: "SON OF A BITCH!"]

"GENGRI"

[DEFINITION: "WHORE"]

"CHONG MANG!"

[DEFINITION: "I DON'T GIVE A FUCK!"]

"GA-REE"

[DEFINITION: "WHORE / SLUT"]

"TOOD-MUEK"

[DEFINITION: "ASSHOLE"]

"GOOK KUAY"

[DEFINITION: "DAMNED PENIS"]

"NA-HEE"

[DEFINITION: "CUNTFACE"]

"AI NA DAD"

[DEFINITION: "CLITFACE"]

"YET PED"

[DEFINITION: "DUCK FUCKER"]

"MAI CHAWP KHUN, DAG LING!"

[DEFINITION: "I DON'T LIKE YOU, MONKEY ASS!"]

HOW TO SWEAR IN
KOREAN

"JI-RAL HA-NE!"

[DEFINITION: "BULLSHIT!"]

"AH, JOT-GAT-NE!"

[DEFINITION: "AH, FEELS FUCKED UP!"]

"GAE-SE-KI-YA!"

[DEFINITION: "YOU SON OF A BITCH!"]

"SHI-BAL-NOM-A!"

[DEFINITION: "YOU MOTHERFUCKER!"]

"SHIBSEKI"

[DEFINITION: "BITCH / WHORE"]

HOW TO SWEAR IN
BENGALI

"KUTTI"

[DEFINITION: "BITCH"]

"JOWHRA"

[DEFINITION: "SLUT"]

"KHANKI / MAGGI"

[DEFINITION: "WHORE"]

"BOKA CHODA BAPER ACHOMKA CHODA CHELE"

[DEFINITION: "SON OF A STUPID FATHER WHO GOT STARTLED WHEN HE WAS BORN"]

"THOR MATHA GOOE BORA!"

[DEFINITION: "YOUR HEAD IS FULL OF SHIT!"]

"AMI TOR DUDHE PESHAB KORBO!"

[DEFINITION: "I'M GOING TO PISS IN YOUR MILK!"]

"TOR MAR DOSHTI BUNI!"

[DEFINITION: "YOUR MOM HAS TEN TITS!"]

"TOR MAA SAGOLER SHATE CHOOD KORE"

[DEFINITION: "YOUR MOTHER HAS RELATIONS WITH GOATS"]

"MOTA KUTTA"

[DEFINITION: "FAT DOG"]

HOW TO SWEAR IN
HINDI

"BADIR / BADIRCHAND / BAKLAND"

[DEFINITION: "IDIOT"]

"BHOOT-NEE KA!"

[DEFINITION: "SON OF A WITCH!"]

"CHINAAL"

[DEFINITION: "WHORE"]

"GHASTI / GASHTI / GASTI / GHASSAD"

[DEFINITION: "HOOKER"]

"CHUTIA / CHUTIYA / CHOO-TIA / CHUTAN"

[DEFINITION: "FUCKER / BASTARD"]

"HARAAMI / HARAAM ZAADA"

[DEFINITION: "BASTARD"]

"KUTTIYA"

[DEFINITION: "BITCH"]

"KHOTEY KI AULAD!"

[DEFINITION: "SON OF A DONKEY!"]

"SAALI KUTTI"

[DEFINITION: "BLOODY BITCH"]

"TATTI"

[DEFINITION: "SHIT"]

HOW TO SWEAR IN PUNJABI

"PAINCHOD"

[DEFINITION: "SISTERFUCKER"]

"MACHOD"

[DEFINITION: "MOTHERFUCKER"]

"TERI PAN DI"

[DEFINITION: "YOU SON OF A BITCH"]

"SAALE"

[DEFINITION: "ASSHOLE"]

"KANJAR DI ULAAD"

[DEFINITION: "SON OF A PIMP"]

"ULLU DA PATTHA"

[DEFINITION: "CHILD OF AN OWL"]

"KHOTTE"

[DEFINITION: "DONKEY"]

"SHADAI / SHADAIN"

[DEFINITION: "A MALE RETARD / A FEMALE RETARD"]

SWEARCLOPEDIA
DIARY

(WRITE DOWN YOUR EXPERIENCES AND REACTIONS FROM USING YOUR NEWLY LIST OF PROFANITY!)

....
....
....
....
....
....
....
....
....
....

Printed in Great Britain
by Amazon

14314458R00058